Acknowledgeme

This book could not have been possible without every person I have met on my life's journey. Each person I have interacted with good or bad has shaped me into the woman I am. It would require a separate book to thank everyone who has made a profound difference in my story, but as you read these words, you know who you are. I dedicate my success to you.

Special thanks to my boyfriend Fidel Marks for my book cover. You can follow his art on Instagram @vipendolupus. Further thanks to a good friend Elle Coffman, who drew the original sketch for my book cover. Thank you both for breathing my words into visual art.

Please understand the contents of this book are not easy to read. Before diving into the pages, make sure you have someone to confide in if you become triggered. This book includes topics substance abuse, self harm, relationship problems, trauma, and alot of vulgar language. If at any time you feel a danger to yourself or others please call 911. It is never to late to get on a better path.

"Sometimes life comes down to surviving. When you survive day after day, eventually one day you realize you are thriving and you made it through."
-Glenaida Mercado J.D.

Prologue

Before checking Herself into psychiatric inpatient, She jots down her fears, or rather her reality.

Her: A 168-hour day would have terrified me, but that seems like a lifetime ago.

I wonder if it's concerning how maniacally mature, I would grow.

But I'm in my 168th hour, and I'm honestly not even scared.

I can't think of any more ways I could possibly be more prepared.

To be honest, I'm just really annoyed...annoyed beyond any measure.

Annoyed at this inconvenience that's denying me any possible pleasure.

Annoyed that my body is failing me when I have the will to survive.

Annoyed that my treatment's not working when I

actually want to be alive.

Annoyed at the possible solution being a hospital stay.

Because if that is the answer, it will happen to go this way.

My son will be so disappointed that I'll have to be gone for 3 weeks.

It won't show in his actions, but you'll tell by the way that he speaks.

My husband will be overwhelmed not knowing if I am okay.

The loneliness will trigger depression, not knowing how long I'll stay.

My parents won't understand why after a year, I am back.

They will wonder if it's for attention or if school is what made me crack.

Now, forget about everyone. Let's talk about me, because my health is what is at risk.

Let's talk about the lovely things I'll have to deal with as me the doctors try to fix.

Finding a doctor to take my case is impossible to say the least.

I'll sit in the ER for 48 hours with Buffalo's finest feast.

The addicts, the drunks, the schizos, and homeless, the clinically insane.

The shit in the corner, the piss on wall, all thanks to my lovely brain.

I'll sit in this room waiting for my evaluation and a
transfer to a long-term floor.

After 12 hours, I'll meet with a doctor and he will ask me what I am here for.

I will tell him I have Bipolar Type 1, and I am having a manic episode.

He will tell me I don't seem manic and it's not
appropriate to self-diagnose.

I will roll my eyes and tell him I've been through this for years.

I haven't slept in 7 days. Believe me...I don't want to be here!

His stupidity will just continue, and I will just get mad.

That mania he denied, well it will harm him quite bad...

I'll be injected with God knows what and wake up like 8 hours later.

Another 12 hours will go by and another doctor, I will cater.

Eventually I'll get to a long-term floor where I will stay indefinitely.

I'll argue with more doctors who think they know my body better than me.

I'll deal with horrible med reactions prolonging my
hospital stay.

Making difficult my virtual education and driving me more insane.

Eventually I'll get out and be on tons of meds that make me feel some type of way.

And I'll just keep doing life until my next 168-hour day.

PART 1

CHAPTER 1

After a guided group meditation, where Her mind palace safe place was blocked off by a "no entry" sign, She drew a picture of sadness in her Heart and chaos in her Brain. There was a blockage preventing the two from communicating. She laid in bed and cried...

Heart: Can you hear me? I don't know what to do...

Brain: I hear your cry, but I don't want the same as you.

Heart: I want her tears to cease; we need to end this hell!

Brain: Tears are not the enemy; She just needs to get well.

Heart: How can She get well when you destroyed what makes Her safe?

Brain: I am not to curse! She was stagnant in that place.

Day after day She would just stay in her mind, the world She tried to flee.

So, I boarded up her safe place, and She returned to reality.

Heart: To the reality you destroy with impulsive decisions?

For caring so much you show a lack of provisions.

She has people who love Her, and you disregard their reactions.

Brain: People will move on; I care for Her satisfaction.

Heart: You're so fucking hard to deal with, why can't we just agree?

Brain: Same to you my dear, but we are both stuck in this body.

She needs to focus on Herself, and disregard other's needs.

Heart: That would be nice, if possible, but on helping others She feeds.

Brain: How can She get better if She puts Herself last?

Heart: That's the million-dollar question and we need to think fast!

Brain: Well, which one of us does forgiveness, it's truly been a while.

Heart: I don't know if I'm even capable; even the word seems quite vile.

Brain: How about we list all that we have tried, to see if it could work again.

Yes, I am capable of working with you; we are stuck here until the end.

Heart: Alright well, I've tried making love and snuggling the kid.

Brain: I've tried fucking all that walks and betting the highest of bid.

Heart: Ummm, I've tried helping others and showering them with gifts!

Brain: I've tried to shield Her from depression with extreme manic lifts.

Heart: FUCK! I think you are right, forgiveness may be it…

Brain: WHAT? We are on the same page for once! Wow, HOLY SHIT!

Heart: Hold your shits. I've only ever forgiven one.

Brain: Beats me love; I've forgiven none.

Heart: She loved Him so much She let anger go.

Brain: She loves Him more than Herself you already know.

Heart: For once we are on the same page with a common goal.

Brain: Now that we are working together, maybe She can feel whole.

Heart: Let's help Her forgive all that She's done.

Brain: Me, You, Her, Together as One!

CHAPTER 2

A puzzle was thrown at Her by another psychiatric patient. To the surprise of many, She just walked away and yelled. However, her Anxiety was severely heightened.

Brain: I couldn't sleep.

Heart: I felt you racing.

Brain: How was I supposed to respond? I can't stop pacing.

Heart: Thank you for choosing to walk away; you put Her first.

Brain: But I didn't release my rage, only making Her worse.

Eyes: Well, I am up early because you two constantly talk. I'm dry, She's fine.

Brain: Back to bed let's walk.

CHAPTER 3

She is improving, but Her anxiety is getting in the way as She agrees to start taking medication. Every past suicide attempt has been while on medication and She feels her body is not able to process the present moment.

Brain: I think She's starting to feel alright,
But She is still not sleeping through the night.
Heart: I have noticed her Anxiety heightened during
conversations.
When things get uncomfortable, I begin racing.
Mouth: When you race, I can't stop talking.
We fuck it all up and in the corner She's rocking.
Brain: Maybe if you could let me think and shut the fuck up. I could process what is being heard.
Ears: Maybe if you paused to hear me, your
interpretations would be less absurd.
Heart: Step 1: recognize the problem.
Brain: The problem is we are fucked!

CHAPTER 4

She explains to a friend that Indifference can be very scary with Bipolar Disorder Type 1. It can be a warning sign that Mania or Depression is starting. On the contrary, it could just mean that She feels "normal".

Brain: Dammit! She's Indifferent, I never know what to do.

Heart: Will She go higher or become Depressed; I don't have a clue.

Brain: In the past, She always spiraled down in Rage or complete Despair.

Heart: It's almost like Indifference and Peace cannot be a pair.

Mouth: Can you two shut the fuck up? Did you not see Her just smile?

Ears: I heard Her laugh.

Heart: I feel love.

Mouth: And I stopped talking for a while!

Heart: Maybe we don't give Her the credit She deserves.

Brain: We were sitting here all anxious, but She calmed Her own nerves

Ears: Yesterday She was told "old Her" is not the goal.

Heart: That's beautifully said because "new Her" will make us whole.

CHAPTER 5

Nighttime can be so scary; that's when demons come to play. Are they real or just in the Brain?

Brain: She's doing really well; I'm scared I'll fuck it up.

Heart: Stay calm my dear and Her life you won't disrupt.

Brain: Even when I'm calm, I feel that I am still racing.

Like I'm going so fast, but all of you are slow pacing.

Heart: With Eyes gently closed it is time to remind us,

Of all that is comforting so Insomnia can't bind us.

Remember the embrace our little monster gave us, and the kiss on the cheek he gave before bed?

Look at this man beside us, we are all that runs through His head.

Brain: Great memories Heart, but if I am being honest, lying next to a man is not comforting to me.

CHAPTER 6

Dealing with medication complications and a flat-out exhausted partner, She was feeling pretty heated as was most of Her body.

Brain: Hands, FUCKING PUNCH HIM. UGH, I'm so MAD!

Hands: We can do that! After impact we'll no longer be sad!

Heart: Oh, stop we love Him so much, Mouth back me up, you love his touch!

Mouth: HOLD THE FUCK UP! There are multiple organs that make up the Mouth.

Tongue: Yeah, ask Tonsils how they feel about touching down south.

Tonsils: I think the bastard deserves to get cussed out!

Tongue: Yeah, only I'll do all the work, while Lips just prance about.

Lips: If it wasn't for me, no one would care about you.
But I think He is great. I just love kisses from Boo!

Brain: Everyone shut up, this is a daily conversation. Let's deck Him, get it done, and save the explanation.

CHAPTER 7

*With starting medication, She has entered a dangerous
Depression with the adjustment period.*

Heart: Is it me who has all this Sadness? I think I am
ruining Her life.
Brain: Oh stop, it is you who loves Him. Remember how close you
held Him last night?
Heart: She loves Him so much; His touch makes me feel whole.
His smile, His satisfaction is always the goal.
Brain: She needs Him I agree.
But we cannot forget.
She needs to get better; Dependency I won't let.
Heart: I understand, tell me your plan.
Brain: Unfortunately, I don't think I can,
Maybe medication is the answer you see,
I think the biggest problem here is me.
My dear, I am Broken and I don't know what to do.
That's why I'm a dick and constantly blaming you.
I send you memories that only cause pain.
I make you cringe; I make you strain.
I see Her Sad and know I'm the one to blame.
Then I send memories of Love;

It's a really sick game.

But sometimes She loves it,

Sometimes She cries.

But I'm scared if it continues,

She will be who dies.

I'm fucked up, Indecisive,

And I think way too much.

I'm sorry I'm so Broken,

I am Her crutch.

Heart: Without you I would be nothing. I wouldn't even beat.

I am what compels Her, but you are Her feat.

She is a wonder woman all because of you.

Just give it some time and we all will make it through.

The medicine will help calm your Anxiety.

She is practicing self-help, a solid remedy.

He really loves Her; I am sorry that I waiver.

I hate to see Her cry,

We are all in Her favor.

CHAPTER 8

Insomnia is a bitch, especially when you can't control it.

Her: Brain, can you shut down, I need to go to bed!

All I can feel is you active in my head.

Brain: But I'm preparing for today you have a lot going on.

Her: I can't do shit if all I do is yawn.

Brain: Fine, if you don't need me, have fun on all your tests.

Her: Ugh you are such a dick I really need my rest. Please and thank you STOP FUCKING RUNNING.

Brain: Touché my dear but don't forget, I'm the one who makes you cunning.

CHAPTER 9

Day three of no sleep.

Heart: Why are you such a dick, I thought we had our talk?

Brain: Yeah, we agreed on time, so until then, the same path I'll walk.

Heart: You are so fucking annoying. How do you drive me Insane?

Brain: Pretty simple; I am the Alpha Brain.

Heart: Motherfucker She needs rest, is sleeping that much of a bore?

Brain: Well we know who She listens to; you are her core.

CHAPTER 10

Mania is full force, only this time it includes extreme
Anxiety and Anger. It is causing problems between Him and Her.

Brain: Heart, are you ok? It feels like we are on the same page.

Heart: NO, I'M NOT OK! All I feel is Rage.

You and Mouth go so fast, I simply can't keep pace.

Then He thinks She doesn't get what it's like to be
common place.

She sounds so smart because of you but none of us know what we
want.

You see me hurt, team up with Mouth and a large
vocabulary you flaunt.

Hands and Feet seem influenced by crack; they can't fucking sit
still.

Brain, why are you triggering us all against our fucking will?

CHAPTER 11

She is feeling the effects of late medication refills and obligation stress at home.

Her: (deep breaths)
There is tension in my Brain, I don't quite know why,
I also feel my Heart hurt. It's like it wants to die.
The rest of me feels normal, my Eyes are sore from tears,
I hope my Body is on one page so we can grow in coming years.

CHAPTER 12

She is in a complete and total Depression. She will not leave her bed and her diet consists of cookies.

Brain: She's getting really slow. She's not stimulating me at all.

Heart: I feel Her falling apart. She's like a crumbling wall.

Ears: He says things to Her without realizing its weight.

Mouth: No matter what I say, his body separates.

Brain: I don't know what He wants, it seems to never be enough.

Heart: Living in this house is getting really tough.

Hands: But the little boy, I've never felt him so content.

Heart: He does feel safe here, but we still lament.

Eyes: I saw Her medication is off, hopefully that can fix Her

Right Arm: She put something in me today, formerly where two scars were.

Ears: Birth control my friend! Uterus, how you feeling?

Uterus: Like shit, this sucks let's get on with the fucking healing.

Back: What about me? I hurt like hell.

Uterus: Finally, someone to share pain with as well.

Brain: This is so overwhelming; I don't know what to do.

Even when we work together, the cracks, She's falling through.

She's supposed to be healing, but She is rapidly getting worse.

Will She ever feel normal or are we all under a curse?

CHAPTER 13

After a disagreement between Her and Him, She slammed both doors and sped out of the driveway.

Heart: Was that an appropriate response?

Brain: I think it was.

Mouth: He doesn't hear us!

Heart: I think He does.

Brain: Great, once again we all disagree,

And then people wonder what's wrong with me.

Heart: Well, maybe we are like them.

Brain: You're the flower, but I am your stem.

Sure, when the flower wilts the stem would like one more lively.

So, it gives the flower nutrients, which then revives it timely.

CHAPTER 14

Her lithium level rapidly drops after the Doctor accidentally prescribes 600mg/day instead of 1200mg/day.

Arm: She keeps cutting and burning me.

Brain: I know, and I'm the one to blame.

I don't know what's wrong with me. I'm so Angry; I'm the flame.

Heart: It's not all your fault, I'm Hopeless. I can't see past today.

Both of us were naive to think our problems would wash away.

Brain: I just want to function the way I should.

To take the blade from Her hand, I wish I could.

But I can't stop the way that I feel.

Unless we get this medicine; She is not going to heal.

Heart: I don't think we can get through this,

I honestly don't think I've ever been so Hopeless.

CHAPTER 15

16 days of insufficient Lithium levels with Doctors not being urgent.

Heart: I can't feel Love or Joy. I'm growing Numb.

Brain: Me too, my dear.

Heart: I feel nothing but Hopelessness.

Brain: I feel nothing but Fear.

Right Arm: Her birth control's out at my expense, you know between the self-harm and doctors, I feel quite tense

Heart: Is this what Death feels like? What's the point of being alive?

Brain: Death is less painful than this; that's why I have tried.

I am Broken, I can't function and it's not even my fault.

The stupid assholes force Her to take medication, Big Pharma is a cult.

Then I am over here hurting the woman I want to grow.

Because they fuck up the medication and now, I function slow.

Heart: God help us, this is the end.

CHAPTER 16

It is a new year and CNA training has started for Her. The medications are more stable but She deals with extreme anxiety. Lithium tremors have begun.

Brain: Well, we are back and shit, I need a drink.

Mouth: It would be nice if you asked consent, but I'm also on the brink.

Heart: Brain, you need to figure this out you have been forgetting so much.

Brain: For some reason, I've lost connection with touch.

Hands why aren't we connecting, I am the Brain.

Hands: You are falling apart and going insane!

We will always hold you up, but this simply will not do.

We are gonna all shut down until you get back to you.

CHAPTER 17

Depression continues. Work and bed are all She knows.

Ears: He's yelling again that we've been in bed for days.

Heart: I can't stop beating I'm growing Enraged.

Eyes: I can't stop crying, I hate when He yells.

Brain: I'm sick of this body and living in hell.

CHAPTER 18

Alcoholism has become Her only comfort.

Her: Body, do you hate me? Why can't I just feel normal?
Why don't we work together? It's all so paranormal.
All I can do is drink to feel like my Feet are on the ground.
Then my Brain's not blowing up and I am safe and sound.

CHAPTER 19

More Anti-psychotics, more Anti-depressants, higher doses, more, more, more...

Heart: See, all Her woes come from you.
Whatever rut you are in, you better get through.
Brain: It's the medication, I swear,
It's like I'm paralyzed and not even here.
Eyes: Her appointment is soon. Until then we wait.
Brain: I'll just feel like shit until then. How motherfucking great.

CHAPTER 20

She was prescribed Depakote, which caused a reaction leading to a week of self-harm. In the bathroom with a razor... what will She do?

Brain: Without me, She dies,
With me, She can't survive.
I'm her best attribute, the Brain,
But I cause Her so much pain.
She bends, I break and run,
I'm terrified of what's to come.
Her Intelligence comes from me,
But not her Strength, it's clear to see.
I am trying so hard to get Her up,
But these drugs keep me trapped inside a torturous cup.
I can't save Her. Will we both die?
She has so much life to live; I can't bear to see Her cry.
I will not be the one to cause all this pain.
I'm sad it's come to this,
Suicide of Brain.

CHAPTER 21

She wakes up at home with scabs on her arm bleeding heavily. She can't recall the events of the previous night. She lays back in bed and falls asleep.

Heart: What the fuck just happened?

Ears: It's like we are losing power.

Legs: We can't get out of bed.

Mouth: Weird She isn't drunk at this hour.

Heart: Brain, buddy, are you there? Can you feel what's going on?
Can you hear my voice, best friend? It feels like you are gone…

Ears: He is gone. I hear nothing…no voices in our head!

Heart: Idiot! That's not good. That means that we are all dead!
I need to pump as hard as I can. This might hurt Her a bit.
But I'm saving her life; ignore her cries. We are in serious shit.
Mouth and Ears keep communicating with Brain. I'm sending him lots of blood.
Arms, Legs, Feet and Hands for a moment you may feel numb.
Pump harder and faster, I know I can do it. Anything for a friend.
I'll pump till I burst, if that's what it takes.
It's me and you till the end.

Brain: Hello? What happened?

Mouth: You died; Heart saved you. Can we skip the hugs?

Brain: I can't believe I took my life. It must have been the drugs.

Heart: Brain, I love you so much! Please don't leave us again.

Only a couple more days than the medication slows and together we will conquer, my friend.

CHAPTER 22

She knows that She needs help. She feels Hopeless and stuck.

Her: I can't continue to live like this.
Will it ever stop?
It's like I feel like flying,
Then my wings fail, and I drop.
But then I'm in the air again.
But only for a short time.
Then I crash back down to earth,
And I stop on the dime.

CHAPTER 23

After months of highs and lows and the decision to once again discontinue medication, She suffers a migraine for one week.

Brain: I can't take this any longer. I feel I'll explode.

Heart: I don't know what I can do to lessen this load.

Hands: I've given mouth pill after pill. If that isn't working, I don't know what will!

CHAPTER 24

Finally, She went to get an infusion for her migraine. She was given 1000mgs of Depacon with a 5-day taper of 500mgs of Depakote. Then immediately She went back to work her overnight shift.

Brain: The pain is gone, but I feel Sad.

Heart: Just keep working, it won't be that bad.

Hands: Says the one who isn't wiping ass all night.

Arms: Or turning residents who are far from light.

Brain: I don't think I am doing alright…

CHAPTER 25

Day three of the Depakote taper.

Arm: Ow what the fuck are you doing to me?

Hand: I can't stop he won't let me free!

Brain: Oh my God, what did I just do? You're bleeding, I forced you to cut all the way through.

Heart: Brain what is going on? The medicine was supposed to help but something has gone wrong.

CHAPTER 26

After 3 days of increasingly deeper cuts, She checks Herself into the Psychiatric Hospital. During her stay She was fired from her job, losing her health insurance. Upon release She had to pay over 3000 dollars for the medication they started Her on.

Her: Why do I keep cutting? Where is the relief?
Is this me or my Brain? I'm in utter disbelief.
I don't want to die, but I want to kill myself.
I don't want to leave my family; I just want to be someone else.
I feel guilty and sad, and I can't take all this pain.
The harder I try to get ahead, the more my efforts seem in vain.
A razor to my arm deep is all I can see.
Blood dripping from my arm as life escapes from me.

PART 2

CHAPTER 27

A year filled with pain so close to death. The next year only held more stress. There was global pandemic followed by political corruption. He married Her, but their first year of marriage held many tears.

Brain: I can't argue any more. Why are people so dumb?
How have their Hearts hardened and become so numb?
Arm: She's gotten better, but I'm still filled with scabs.
Brain: They still can't figure it out even after all these labs.
Heart: Guys, I'm nervous this seems like a lifelong war.
Brain: Well, I will fight to the end because I know life has more.
She isn't just anyone; She is so unique.
Her lack of self-love is all I would tweak.
Heart: She has to get through this I know She can.
We will not leave Her, nor will Her man.

CHAPTER 28

Depression sinks in, self-harm and drinking increase.

Ears: She's been going to church and talking to those ladies.

Eyes: She has been reading the scripture even more than daily.

Mouth: She says She's ok and her faith is so strong.

Arm: Well, She keeps cutting me, so something is wrong.

Brain: Guys, I'm so sorry. I'm still such a mess.

I don't know why I bring Her so close to death.

Why can't they help me? What is the cure?

I can't keep hurting Her. I need to remember all that we were.

CHAPTER 29

Her husband is growing more concerned. He is scared She will have to go to the hospital.

Brain: What should I do? What do I say?
No matter my choices, it ends up this way.
I'm always leading Her back then they dope Her up on meds.
When I say this, I mean it. We can't do this again!
We can't be trapped in that hell.
We can't be made to feel well.
God, please help us. We need you! Can you even tell?

CHAPTER 30

She realizes that in order to survive, She needs a completely new direction in life. She decides to apply for law school.

Heart: Those who can't, teach. I can be the change I wish to see.
Since I've failed miserably at changing me.
Brain: How the fuck are you gonna take credit? That test score was all me.
I blew through those logic games with effortless simplicity.
Hands: Yeah, because you typed in every letter.
Eyes: He couldn't even see the words, if I wasn't trapped in his fetter.
Heart: Guys! We all made this happen; we are a team.
Maybe our future is brighter than it may seem.

CHAPTER 31

A letter from the University at Buffalo arrives in the mail.

Eyes: HOLY SHIT! She made it!!!! She got into law school!
Brain: What? She got a scholarship? Oh, this will be cruel.
Heart: C'mon think positive, I'm sure it will be great.
Hands: The future is painful hell, that's all I anticipate.
Heart: Maybe this journey is exactly what we need.
A new start, a new life, her soul we can feed.

CHAPTER 32

He mopes in the basement. She doesn't know what to do, Exhausted.

Heart: He is Depressed again. This is so exhausting.

Brain: He is Paranoid beyond belief and her Patience it is costing.

Heart: She doesn't see Him as a loser, that's just how he sees Himself.

Brain: Why can't he just see She has Him on the highest shelf?

Heart: I can't do this anymore; each day gets more Depressing.

Brain: Each day they grow more in Denial of the Rage are each suppressing.

CHAPTER 33

She expresses She needs space. A fight rapidly unfolds. He moves the bed into the basement.

Heart: Wow that was really bad. Should we go check on Him?

Brain: No, it will make it worse. His tolerance is very thin.

Heart: I CAN'T STAND IT WHEN HE FEELS LIKE THIS.

Brain: Well, She's a victim too,

What we say He'll just dismiss.

Then what can She do?

Mouth: We hurt, Throats not doing so well.

Throat: I'm gonna need some sleep. I'm raw and red as hell.

Heart: Is it always gonna be like this, miscommunication that leads to a fight?

Brain: No this is not sustainable. Unfortunately, I see an end in sight.

CHAPTER 34

She starts her first day of law school. Immediately, She finds a group of people She clicks with.

Heart: Oh my God! I'm gonna burst. Finally, people who see my worth.

Brain: No one gives a damn about you; I'm the only reason that we've pulled through.

Body: Y'all aren't the only two organs here. And y'all argue more than you volunteer.

Brain: Without me none of you would even exist; and She certainly wouldn't be the baddest bitch.

Heart: Can we not be all hostile? This is a huge day. Can we work together and make sure She slays?

CHAPTER 35

She gets a call. Her uncle is having a stroke, She rushes over to help.

Brain: Eyes, Hands, find all his prescriptions and put them in this bag.

Heart, stay strong, you can do this, put down your white flag.

Lungs, keep breathing deep you control the Body now.

Everyone you're doing great; I hope he makes it through somehow.

Ears: I hear the helicopter; I hope they save his life.

Heart: I hope our love meant enough to Him to heal all his strife.

CHAPTER 36

Her uncle is revived and able to speak, but something feels off.

Mouth: "Uncie I love you. I love you so much."

Hands: His nerves must be shot. He seems in pain from my touch.

Heart: Brain, what's this feeling? It's so hard to explain.

Brain?: Darling, don't worry. Soon time will end his pain.

Heart: Brain! Where are you and who is this deceiver?

Brain: It's not deception. I'm still Brain, just with a

different receiver.

You can call me Intuition, I'm more fluid than the Brain you know.
I'm the part of the Brain which resonates with you. I'm the empathy you show.

I've always been here, but I rarely take the lead.

However, you'll see more of me now that you're in need.

See, I'm a power beyond explanation, the rest of Brain not comfortable with me yet.

But I'm in charge of your future, and comfortable you will all get.

Heart: Ok, so why take the lead now? Why before did you hide?

Intuition: I'm here now, so we can't deny. Uncie is already on the other side.

Say your goodbyes and hold our family close.

Make sure Uncie knows we all love Him the most.

This will not be easy, but his suffering will end.

It will be hardest for little monster to lose his best friend.

CHAPTER 37

Grieving the death of Uncie, stressed about fights with Him, exhausted from comforting a grieving child, overwhelmed with law school readings, She receives a text from a family member criticizing Her as a wife and mom.

Heart: This stupid jealous ass salty bitch!
I should kick her ass until her face needs a stitch.
Brain: Heart calm the fuck down, it's really not that serious.
That woman's jealousy of us is just making her Delirious.
We aren't perfect for little monster or even for Him.
But she has no right to text us solely on a whim.
Pay attention to her words. She doesn't feel enough.
So, she wants to spread her weaknesses in hopes that we give up.
They all want us to fail only to say, "I told you so."
But we will be victorious, and one day they will know.
Heart: Ugh, I'm so confused. Is this my Brain or Intuition?
Brain: It's me darling; ignore that superstition.
Heart: You sound just like her though, do I need to be concerned?
Brain: Nah, it's fine. I'm here now. Let's make sure this bitch gets burned.
Hands: (types a witty response back).

CHAPTER 38

After a strange night, She receives alarming news.

Heart: Brain! Something is wrong. I don't know what to do.

Eyes: Something's very wrong. I can't stop searching for drugs to pursue.

Mouth: Grab some Klonopin, we can't stay in this state.

Brain: What the fuck is happening why are you all irate?

Heart: SOMETHING IS WRONG, I think I want to die?

Lungs: No, we are dying, I just don't know why.

Brain: Guys! What is happening; I don't know what to do!?!?

Hands: Mouth take these pills; we're going to have to sleep this through.

Ears: Guys, wake up. The phone is blowing up.

Eyes: Oh... Oh my.... Her whole town this will disrupt.

CHAPTER 39

She doesn't know how to feel after receiving a text, Her classmate committed suicide.

Intuition: Brain is taking a bit of rest to process what happened last night.

It's ok if you all feel confused, it was definitely a fright.

But Brain is rapidly expanding into more than the hyper-rational Brain you know.

Empathy and Intuition will begin to run the show.

With Brain rapidly developing, acclimating will be hard.

Just remember Brain is still here, but of *their* growth please have regard.

Empathy: Last night, I was the reason everyone felt insane.

I wish I had more control over feeling people's pain.

I'm sorry that I hurt everyone, I'm very new to this.

Understanding how other's feel is way more harm than bliss.

CHAPTER 40

Law school is getting more intense. Arguments in the house are getting more intense. Everything in Her life is going wrong. Delayed Grief sets in, and Existentialism takes over.

Her: Father, why have you forsaken me,
Tell me what more will you take from me?
Because I don't think I can handle it,
Every time I build you dismantle it.
Father, you told me you'd hear my prayer,
Why when I cry out are you not there?
This is too much weight for me to take,
You could hold it all, but you watch me break.
Father, why have you forsaken me?
Intuition: Darling, you can't do this alone. Please call and get the help you need.
Your Brain cannot comprehend what is necessary to proceed.

CHAPTER 41

She goes to the hospital to get help for Her existential crisis. She is met with verbal abuse and medical neglect from doctors. She is denied treatment until She makes an attempt on Her life.

Her: I can't do this any longer.

I wish my faith was getting stronger.

But I watch it fade away.

Everyday feels so much longer,

So, I pour my drinks much stronger, until they numb my pain.

I don't think that I want to die.

Oh, I just can't seem to find the answers why.

Round and round and round I go,

The woes of life, they never slow.

I think that I maybe need some help.

I know I need to put that bottle back on that shelf.

But I don't think I could ever let it go.

If I put the bottle down then I'm all alone.

Human, human, Here I am;

I want to be a better man.

I crumble and I fall sometimes and lately I don't feel alive.

Mortal, mortal, self-destruct.

I cannot build, I just corrupt.

I can't seem to find a thrill.
Maybe it's in one last pill.

CHAPTER 42

She gets home from the hospital with no will to participate in life.
Stuck between not wanting to die, but not wanting to live.

Heart: Guys, it's been three days of us barely getting by.

Pill after pill, drink after drink, we can't do this until we die.

I'm Sad, I'm Hurt, I'm so Lonely without Brain.

We were a team and now he's gone Insane.

Our story is not finished, we must reckon this hell.

When we get back on our feet it won't matter that we fell.

CHAPTER 43

She can't stop sobbing remembering everyone who ever hurt Her.

Heart: Brain! I feel you! Are you ok?

Brain: Heart, leave now you can't see me this way!

Heart: Brain don't run. I need you so much.

Brain: Until I process this Trauma, I'm only a crutch.

CHAPTER 44

Sometimes Demons have the loudest voices.

Trauma: Go cry in the corner. You're stupid and useless...just a piece of shit.

You did this to yourself. You burned all your bridges, now you can't handle it.

So, sob at the top of your lungs and bleed till you're numb.

Each cut is one step to mercy where all your pain is done.

You cannot fix this. You fucked up, admit it. Now there's no turning back.

You made your choices. You won't be forgiven. No drugs could cover that...

Heart: Brain....this isn't you.

You are forgiven, we know what you've been through.

We love you...

CHAPTER 45

Even at Her lowest, none can match Her strength.

Heart: Brain, I know we are broken. And I know we will always be.

But if I didn't have you, there would be no me.

We self-destruct and corrupt,

But we always get up.

I won't let today be the end of our story.

We will survive this,

Please don't ignore me.

CHAPTER 46

Empty pill bottle, empty tequila bottle, now what?

Her: God, I don't know what to do,
All I know is I've been failed by you.
You've been negligent, and now I put you on trial,
You allowed the world to hurt me, my body defile,
Why did you let me suffer all that pain?
And everyone I love, tell me it's in my Brain.
I trusted you and had faith all of my life,
But you allowed me to be traumatized by constant strife.
Bullied for my race, nowhere to belong,
Never good enough, wondering what I did wrong.
Never skinny enough to please family,
Constantly belittled for just being me.
Threatened with hell for being pregnant from rape.
The scars on my arm, my only escape.
You are good all the time, all the time you are good?
So, did I deserve all this? I've never understood.
You had a duty to protect me, to keep me in your hand,
But you breached your duty, left me in quicksand.
The damages I incurred, swallowed by abuse.
You didn't even help as I strung up a noose.

As your child, to feel safe is all I've ever wanted,

But instead, you left me abandoned, terrified and haunted…

God: I know…

CHAPTER 47

What does one do when they win their lawsuit? They move on....

Lungs: Guys! Something is wrong,
There is a large hole in me, something is gone.
It happened after She said that really deep prayer.
It was like a hand ripped a hole in me leaving me bare.
Heart: Lungs breathe, I know something has changed,
But please just stay calm, as we get rearranged.
Brain, are you there, love? We really need you now.
Intuition: Heart, I am here. Let me explain to you how.
Brain has been going through some noticeable changes,
You've met Empathy, Trauma and Myself, as Brain
rearranges.
Brain will come back, but we will stay here.
But I promise it's good, there is nothing to fear.
Brain had a breakthrough last night,
It's remarkable to say the least.
He overcame Trauma, an impossible beast.
Lungs, you feel empty, because a weight has been lifted.
Everyone, take a day to rest, then accept what you've been gifted.
Heart: Yeah, that makes a lot of sense, I hope Brain is doing ok.
I think it would be great, if you and Empathy stay.

Brain will need support on this new journey we trek.
We become pretty useless when we both are a wreck.

CHAPTER 48

She is still processing the other night. However, her focus has shifted to finishing the semester.

Brain: Alright everybody, time to get to work!
On these finals we are about to go berserk!
Heart: I'm so happy we are back, I've missed you beyond measure.
I never thought you being bossy would ever bring me pleasure.
Brain: I'm glad we're back, too. I think our future is bright.
We were in darkness for so long, but we made it to the light.

CHAPTER 49

She finished her first year of Law School with just under a 3.0. She started her internship and two summer classes.

Hands: I am so sick of typing, I'm about to have carpal tunnel.
Brain: I'm so sick of thinking, I need a 6 pack through a funnel.
Eyes: Just let me rest and not open for day,
All this blue light has me in a blind haze.
Heart: Ugh all you guys need to quit complaining,
We are living the dream, and it needs no explaining!

CHAPTER 50

After a month of working full time at her internship and completing six law school credits in six weeks, exhausted She submits her final projects, confident She will finally have a B average, 3.0.

Brain: Guys, I think we did it! We got through our first year.
We definitely hit rock bottom, but it's only up from here.
Who would have ever thought we would make it to law school.
And we are a third of the way done; this is so cool.
Heart: We believed in Her, and She believed in us.
We all worked together and got an A minus and B plus.

CHAPTER 51

All good things come to an end. Facing clear discrimination at her first internship, she feels rage and defeat. She remembers her motto, expectations always lead to disappointment.

Brain: Heart, calm me down. I'm about to snap.

How is she gonna talk to Her like that and not expect me to react?

Talking to Her like She is a child, and not a remarkable grown-ass boss.

She should smack her and tell her to fuck all the way off.

Heart: Brain, I am here, but right now you need Empathy.

You are right, she is a bitch, but from another lens let's see.

Empathy: Thank you, Heart, for the referral, Brain I'm here,

Let me try to explain, and unpack this dear.

She talked to Her like that out of her own insecurity,

Because if given the chance, she knows our girl will lead.

Being a queer, disabled woman of color is not fun,

She will always be a target for those She's outdone.

Heart: But this is so discouraging. We were doing so well!

Are we ever going to escape this cycle, our endless hell?

PART 3

CHAPTER 52

She starts Her second year of law school. She is Co-President of the Native and Indigenous Law Students Association, Vice President of the Latin American Law Students Association;, President of Parents and Law Students, Diversity Equity Inclusion Officer of Black Law Students Association and OUTLaw, and a Student Attorney for the Civil Rights and Transparency Clinic. She volunteers for the first-year law students' orientation.

Heart: OH MY GOD. I'm so excited! She is a super star.

Brain: I knew if She kept pushing, we would all go so far.

Heart: The recognition She's receiving, no other student could beat.

Brain: Well, when you always get back up, you can't be conquered by defeat.

Heart: She has so many friends who show up to support.

Brain: She finally feels belonging, peace and comfort.

CHAPTER 53

She understands what it feels like to be an introvert.

Heart: I'M SO FUCKING EXHAUSTED, WHAT THE HELL DO I DO!?!?!

Brain: What? You have a social limit? Oh my God, who knew?

Heart: This isn't funny, Brain! This doesn't feel right.

Being around others used to only fuel my light.

I just want to get away and be alone to just recharge.

I don't know how to handle this predicament at large.

Brain: It's ok, dear, to mature. We know I've matured a lot.

Sometimes extroverts get exhausted and give introversion a shot.

Heart: But it's so different than who I was before,

My sociability is what everyone knows me for.

Brain: I promise you dear; you are still one of a kind.

Take a deep breath and listen to your mind.

CHAPTER 54

She writes a reflection paper in the Civil Rights and Transparency Clinic setting her goals for the semester.

Her: I want to change the world, but I'll take it step by step.

But I suck at time management, so better I should get.

I hope I am good at communicating, ok well I will just put that I am.

I'm a great team player because I actually give a damn!

Oh, and I want to improve my writing, you know do real lawyer stuff.

Shit, why does this reflection feel like it's a bluff?

CHAPTER 55

Her and Him have been living separate for a few months now. She finally realizes their relationship will never work.

Heart: Brain, I don't like this. I miss the old me.

Why is life so much harder when you can finally see?

Brain: Because Ignorance is bliss, as Knowledge leads to action.

Life is harder when we don't live for momentary satisfaction.

Heart: I'm just not ready for change yet, but I know it must be done.

I just feel like an imposter whose understood by no one.

Brain: Just because you know what the future holds doesn't mean there is a specific time frame. One step at a time my dear, don't let this be a mind game.

Heart: When did you get so calm and sensible, Brain? It's just so weird.

I can't believe you were once a Brain we Feared.

CHAPTER 56

School becomes overwhelming as She has to log 20 hours of Clinic work a week on top of reading. Hands are singing, Brain's last nerve is ringing.

Hands: I'm so fucking sick of life every day.

I wish a fucking bomb would blow me all away.

Brain: What the hell are you singing, don't you feel I am stressed enough?

Hands: Not everything is about you, this school shit is tough.

Every day I type, I text, I write.

I have to be on guard 24/7 prepared for any fight.

I have to catch Her when She falls and let's face it

everyone else too.

You will never understand the labor-intensive shit I

always do!!!!

Brain: Carry on....

CHAPTER 57

She volunteers at a free legal services clinic and helps community members write court documents.

Mouth: I haven't smiled this much in years.

Eyes: I have to fight back tears.

Heart: I feel so fulfilled.

Brain: Wow guys...I'm truly thrilled.

Look how far we have come.

It feels like we truly won.

We are here substantially helping our community.

We've grown into the change we've always wished to see.

CHAPTER 58

He never seems to want to talk about the things She wants to talk about.

Ears: All I ever do is listen, but Mouth, He never listens to you.

Mouth: Honestly, there's nothing left to say. This relationship is through.

Heart: I can't bear to lose Him, but I unfortunately agree.

But I don't know if I'm ready for change. It truly terrifies me....

CHAPTER 59

She moves into an apartment with her best friend, a conservative white male. Although opposite in every way, She feels safer than ever before.

Brain: I feel like I can finally breathe,
No arguments to derail me.
Heart: We are finally processing the last few years,
We've changed so much that much is clear.
Hands: I'm just happy to see hands that work much harder than I do.
It's a shame what those motherfuckers are regularly put through.
Heart: Hands, watch your mouth. When did you become so vulgar?
Hands: When I got pissed off and decided not to hold it in any longer.
Y'all speak of growth like it's all for the better,
But I've grown restless from the bullshit we seem to always weather.
This home is our only peace, everything else is shit.
School is insane. We are broke as fuck, and I can't handle it.
I'm constantly texting, hustling on the phone, typing papers on end.

Getting fingernails dug into me as calm She tries to pretend.

I'm sick of Her being anxious and burying that shit cause of you.

So, the next motherfucker to cross me is gonna get a taste of what I've been through.

Mouth: I fully support.

Brain: Hmm can't argue.

Heart: Guys this isn't helpful.

CHAPTER 60

Her last semester of law school commences. She meets someone in the prime of her stress.

Heart: Hands, who are you texting? What happened? You aren't rachet anymore?

Hands: Bitch, fuck you. Wait and see what's in store.

Eyes: Holy Moly, He is cute. I think I'm obsessed.

Brain: Calm down, everybody. I don't know if I'm impressed.

Heart: I like His 90s smiley faces, and it's cute that He doesn't use Emojis.

Hands: I wonder what his hands feel like, I think I want them to hold me.

Brain: Patience everyone, I'm not ready for this again.

Y'all are moving too quick. Can we please just start with "friend"?

CHAPTER 61

No one ever listens to Brain. She starts dating Viper. The relationship takes a lot of work as broken people aren't perfect, but She is happier than She has ever been.

Heart: Brain, I really love Him, I know you struggle to feel the same.

I know you wish you didn't overthink, but you are protecting us from pain.

However, I want you to relax a little, and enjoy the smiles as they come.

I've never seen Mouth so happy, and hopefully Hand's hood rat days are done.

Brain: I wouldn't be so sure about that. If anything, Hands just got worse.

Did you see them ready to fight the other day? And Mouth came in quick to curse.

Heart: Oh...haha yeah. That might have been my fault.

I got a little jealous and that was the result...

Brain: That's why I can't relax dear. The way you guys are acting makes me worry.

I like to keep a clear view, but this love shit makes things blurry.

Heart: So, channel Intuition, she's apart of you for a reason,
Choosing to shut her out feels like an act of treason.
Brain: I want to let her speak, but I'm scared Heart it's true.
I know Intuition is always right, but I'm scared she might hurt you.
Heart: You know me more than anyone, that's why you are my Brain.
You also know my strength and that I can handle a little pain.
My love we are still young we have so much hurt left to endure,
Don't focus so much on pain, that you miss out on love that's pure.
Brain: I'll try to loosen up.

CHAPTER 62

She is off her pedestal. She doesn't feel the desire to ever step back on.

Heart: I think I got my hopes up that a happy ending was in store.

Brain was right, I am weak, this pain I can't endure.

I won't ever be secure enough and not seek everyone's approval.

The only way to protect myself is walls and self-removal.

Brain: I never called you weak. That is a Delusion beyond compare.

Heart, this is one bad moment. Don't fall apart now, don't you dare.

I'm sorry I have been so focused and haven't been giving you the relief you need.

We are going to get better, forward we'll proceed.

CHAPTER 63

She begins studying for the Bar and no one is doing well.

Intuition: Attention Everyone! I have an announcement to make.

I'm going to give a statement, then I'm taking a much needed break.

I know we will get through the next two months in time,

But it's not going to be easy, we will all soon walk the line.

I need you all to work together, even when you have nothing left.

We are entering survival mode, and we cannot waste a single breath.

Everyone report your commitments until we reach the Bar.

Brain, will be working overdrive, don't let your work be subpar.

Heart: I'll keep us moving forward, distracted by Viper when need be.

If any of you need hope, don't hesitate to call on me.

I know sometimes I waiver, but I understand the stakes.

She deserves success and we will do whatever it takes.

Hands: I will do what's necessary with or without Heart's approval,

I will help Brain get through Bar prep and serve as inconvenience removal.

Mouth: I guess my duties depend on how much trouble Hands cause,

But I'll follow direction of Brain and Heart and try to help Hands pause.

Ears: I'm gonna try to focus, I want to support Brain.

I know I'm easily distracted but listening to lectures I'll remain.

Eyes: I actually hate all of you, I can't describe the pain I'm in.

Glasses, eye drops, nothing works, not even medicine.

You think that I can do this? Stare at a screen on end?

You think I give a fuck about the happy dreams y'all pretend.

This is fucking stupid. I'm about to rest.

I'll be here to participate, but don't expect my best.

Brain: You speak like you have ever been this Body's top performer.

Nose, do you smell Insecurities? Ahh, now we are getting warmer.

The fact is you have been deficient since She was in the 6th grade.

This Body has always picked up your slack and fixed mistakes you made.

The great thing about all of this is you report to me.

You can protest all you want, but when I say see, you see.

Heart: That was hott!

CHAPTER 64

She isn't doing well, but She will survive.

Her: I've never wanted to die so much,
But still want to live.
To find relief from anxiety,
There's nothing I wouldn't give.
I am exhausted and burnt out.
I don't have any spoons.
How long have I been like this?
It seems like many moons.
I have this debilitating feeling,
That this still won't be enough.
What if I fail this exam,
Will I still pretend I'm tough?
I don't think anyone understands,
How truly weak I feel.
I can't sleep, I can't breathe,
I can barely finish a meal.
I'm so thankful I found love,
I think it's keeping me alive.
But I've been so distant from my Child.
But it's necessary to survive.

I hope He understands,
I'm doing all this for His good.
I'll make it up to Him soon,
As I know I should.

CHAPTER 65

She takes the Bar Exam. Is it over?

Brain: I actually don't know what to say. I can't believe it's done.

Hands: Wow, we did better than I could have imagined. Shit, there is a chance we may have won?

Heart: Let's not get our hopes up, but we did the best we could. Even if we didn't pass, we still did fucking good.

Hands: We did do good, Heart. Thanks for keeping up our morale. We couldn't have killed it without you. Thanks for keeping me corralled.

Heart: I'm sorry if I made you feel like your actions were out of line.

You have been through a lot over the years, and it's not fair of me to whine.

You are perfect the way you are, and I should not police your expression.

You are a vital part of this Body, and I love our communal progression.

Intuition: I'm so proud of all of us.

CHAPTER 66

One would think the Bar is the finish line, but it's an unlocked door to Hell.

Eyes: I FUCKING HATE ALL OF YOU! WHY AM I CURSED TO THIS HELL?

Brain: You complain so much for someone who is useless as well.

Hands: In Eyes defense, when will we catch a fucking break?

If I'm being honest, I don't know how much more I can take.

So many documents, so many stupid tests, and She can't even be admitted now over a stupid technicality at best?

Brain: I know it's all bullshit, especially when we worked this hard,

But we are so close, we just need to focus and all

distractions discard.

Uterus: I'm not doing so well.

Lungs: I think something is wrong.

Heart: I don't think he loves me!

Brain: FUCKKKKKKKKKKKKKKKK

CHAPTER 67

The two months after the Bar exam are living hell. To graduate She must complete 520 hours of Pro Bono legal work. She gets a horribly painful urgent surgery on her uterus for a condition called adenomyosis. The first three weeks of recovery are incredibly painful. As She starts to
recover and catch up on hours, She develops severe Pneumonia and has a bleeding left lung. She is hospitalized for five days.

Heart: I seriously can't stop laughing. Why is our life a joke?
Lungs: Don't laugh too hard, I'm one chuckle away from a choke.
Eyes: Choke, do it. I'm ready to die.
Brain: Eyes shut the fuck up, your bitch ass doesn't need even one reason why.
Guys, it's a day in the life. It sucks but we will be fine.
Just keep pushing forward and it will get better in time.
Lungs: I could use a cigarette.
Brain: Sounds delightful, but dude we are never smoking again.

CHAPTER 68

He's the one.

Heart: Brain, can I ask you a question?

Brain: Yes, my dear?

Heart: Have you changed your mind about Him?

Brain: I don't think it's quite that clear.

He was never the issue it's more the relationship itself.

Him and Her together merging the cards they've been dealt.

They each carry so much Trauma and don't have the best communication skills.

It can get unhealthy quick when fights start from cheap thrills.

Heart: Mouth has worked really hard to monitor their tone.

They act like they don't care, but Empathy's progress has shown

Brain that personal development all comes from you.

6 years ago, this relationship wouldn't have worked, but now her dreams are coming true.

It's not perfect at all and they both still have much work to put in.

But He loves Her, and they are trying, and this is better than they've ever been.

Brain: I was worried for a moment. I thought She needed to leave.

But when I saw His reaction, I could feel you bleed.

I realized it wasn't Him that was causing your pain but me.

He really is Her endgame, something even Eyes can see.

CHAPTER 69

The Bar results are in.

....

....

....

Eyes: I think She passed.

Brain: What do you mean think?

Eyes: I don't know there are so many words.

Brain: Get your shit together. BLINK!!!

Eyes: Holy shit. Holy shit. HOLY SHIT. She passed and with a pretty high score!

Heart: Holy Fuck! We did it. We don't have to study anymore!

Brain: I'm so proud, but I'm stunned.

Mouth: I'm at a loss for words.

Heart: Let's take time to process, and just be grateful for our girl.

CHAPTER 70

After 10 years of college, She is finished. She's proud but there is a pain deep inside. She pulls out her journal for the first time in a long time.

Her: One would think the last day of law school would call for celebration,

But I can't express the way I feel, though it's surely not elation.

I've completed the impossible, and I know I should be proud,

But deep inside a young girl cries, I hear her screams so loud.

Because She was perfect the way She was, She didn't need a trophy to prove,

That She was worthy, as She was judged for every step and every move.

She would have been enough completing high school at seventeen.

And She did this with a baby then got an Associate's degree.

She survived decades of racism, verbal, and physical abuse,

She survived all the traumas foster care induced.

She was stripped of everything, family, culture, and her name,

She was silenced for years as the world invalidated her pain.

As an adult She tried to listen to the advice everyone gave.

She found Herself a husband, as stability would make her son behave.

She went to church every week to wash away her sin.

She just wanted to be enough, time and time again.

But She was always enough, She was inspirational, brave and smart.

But so many showered Her with hate and ripped her soul apart.

No matter what She did the world was always so critical,

So, She figured a Juris Doctor would hopefully be pivotal.

Now She is me, accomplished yes, but traumatized and broke.

I'm standing at the finish line, and it all feels like a joke.

I feel like I shouldn't be here, despite being glad that I am.

But the only reason I did this was to prove to the world that I can.

I just want to climb inside and hold the little girl as She screams.

And tell Her, fuck everyone and follow your own dreams.

Heart: I'm worried for Her.
Brain: She will be ok.

CHAPTER 71

She gets pre-approved for a mortgage and begins looking for a home for her developing family.

Heart: I never thought I would see forever with a man.

Brain: Yes, I don't particularly like them, but with this one I also can.

Heart: We finally have a chance to have our dream family.

A son, a stepdaughter, and maybe child number three.

Uterus: Hold up. Are we forgetting what I just went through?

Heart: Girl, you'll survive I'm ready for round 2.

Brain: Can we get a house first before y'all decide to make us broke?

Uterus: Y'all? You're the one who drinks excessively and thinks contraception is a joke.

Brain: Ouch.

Eyes: Guys! Email! SHE GOT THE JOB!!!!!!!!

This is so incredible I think I might sob.

Brain: It's good to see you happy Eyes, maybe this can be a new leaf.

It's gonna be a lot of screen time, but we are here when you need relief.

Eyes: I'm sorry I've been an asshole. I will work on it, I swear.

Brain: Happens to the best of us, I also sometimes go there.

Heart: I can't believe how far we have come; it's remarkable to say the least.

She's become a goddess, not many can tame their beasts.

Brain: She started adulthood as a teen mom, spent years in and out of psych wards.

Got her shit together, four degrees and tons of awards.

She's about to be a lawyer, own a home, and have a great job.

It's scary to think that all of these things suicide could have robbed.

Mouth: She's gonna make a difference and I am going to help.

She has answers people need, She knows how to utilize what's been dealt.

She is gonna save lives, She might destroy some too.

But She became a badass because of each and every one of you.

Heart: She wouldn't have made it through any stage of life without her big ass mouth.

EPILOGUE

She finally figured it out.

Her: Tears are the water,
And I am the Earth.
The water will flow,
Until I find my worth.
When worth is found,
A flower will bloom.
And for this new blossom,
The world will make room.
Even if it doesn't,
The bloom will still flourish.
Thanks to years of pruning,
And countless tears to nourish.
My tears were never wasted,
Not one single drop.
Because I became me.
Full Stop.

Made in the USA
Middletown, DE
23 August 2024

59086064R00060